CHRISTMAS COLORING BOOK

Santas In The City

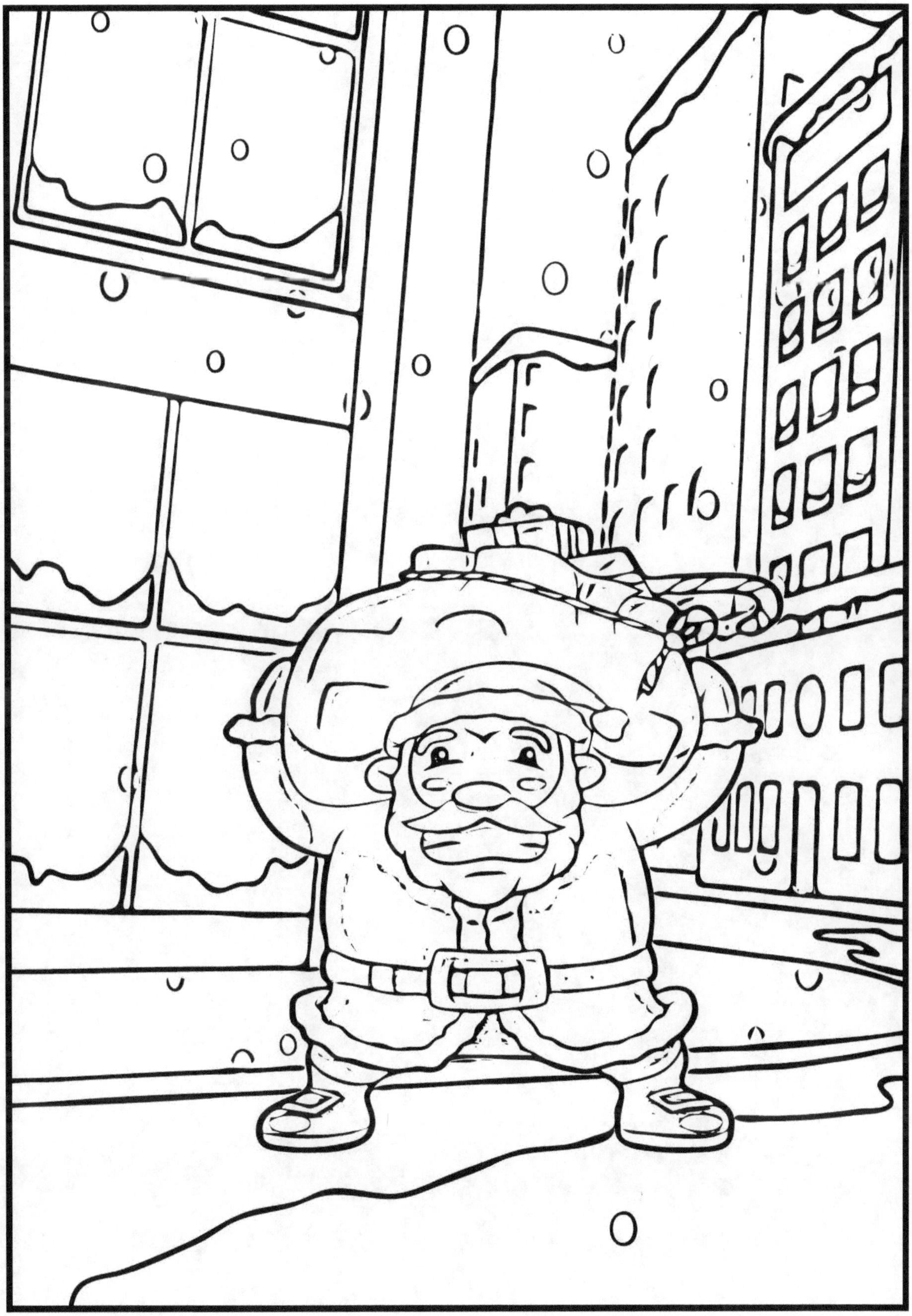

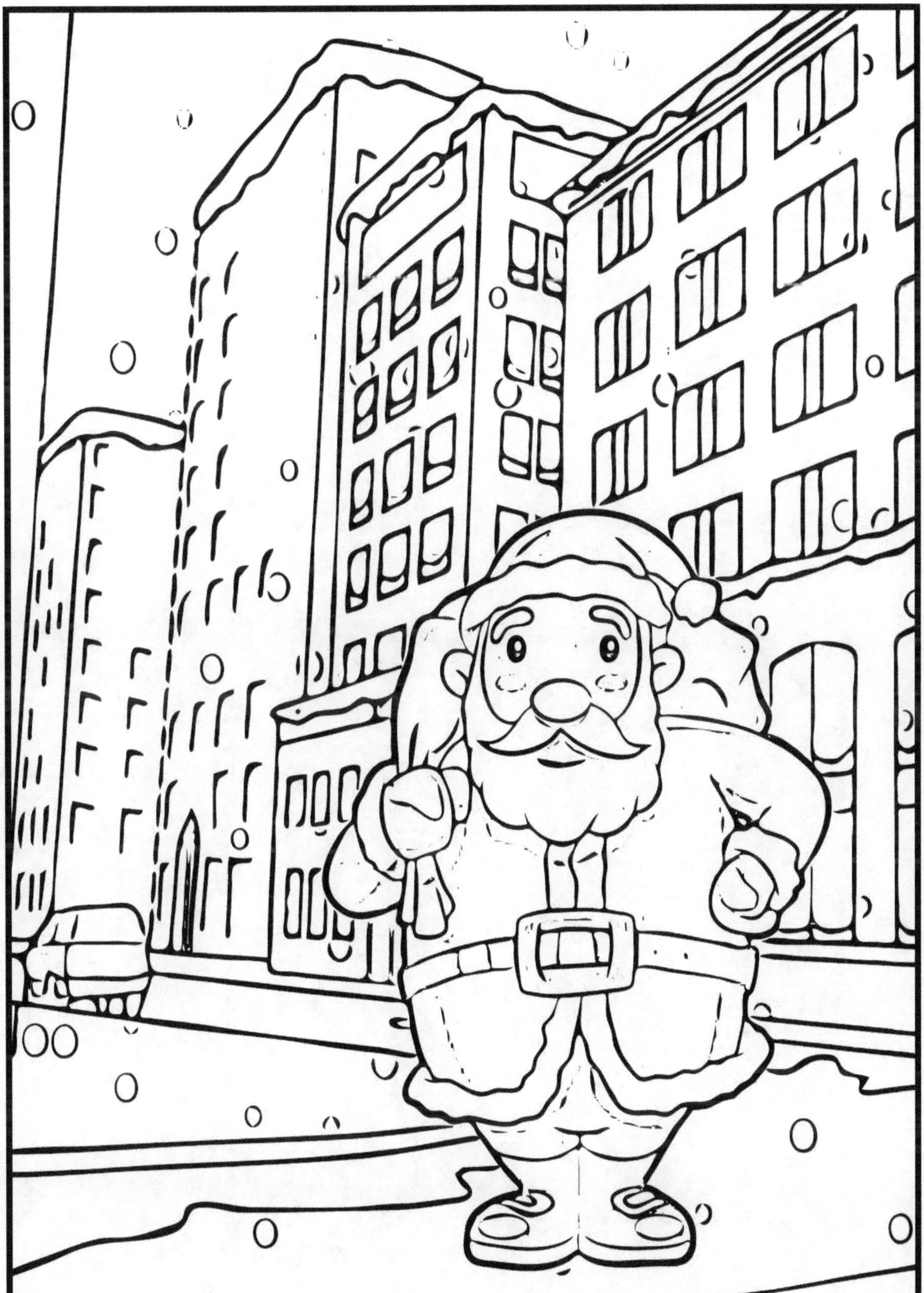

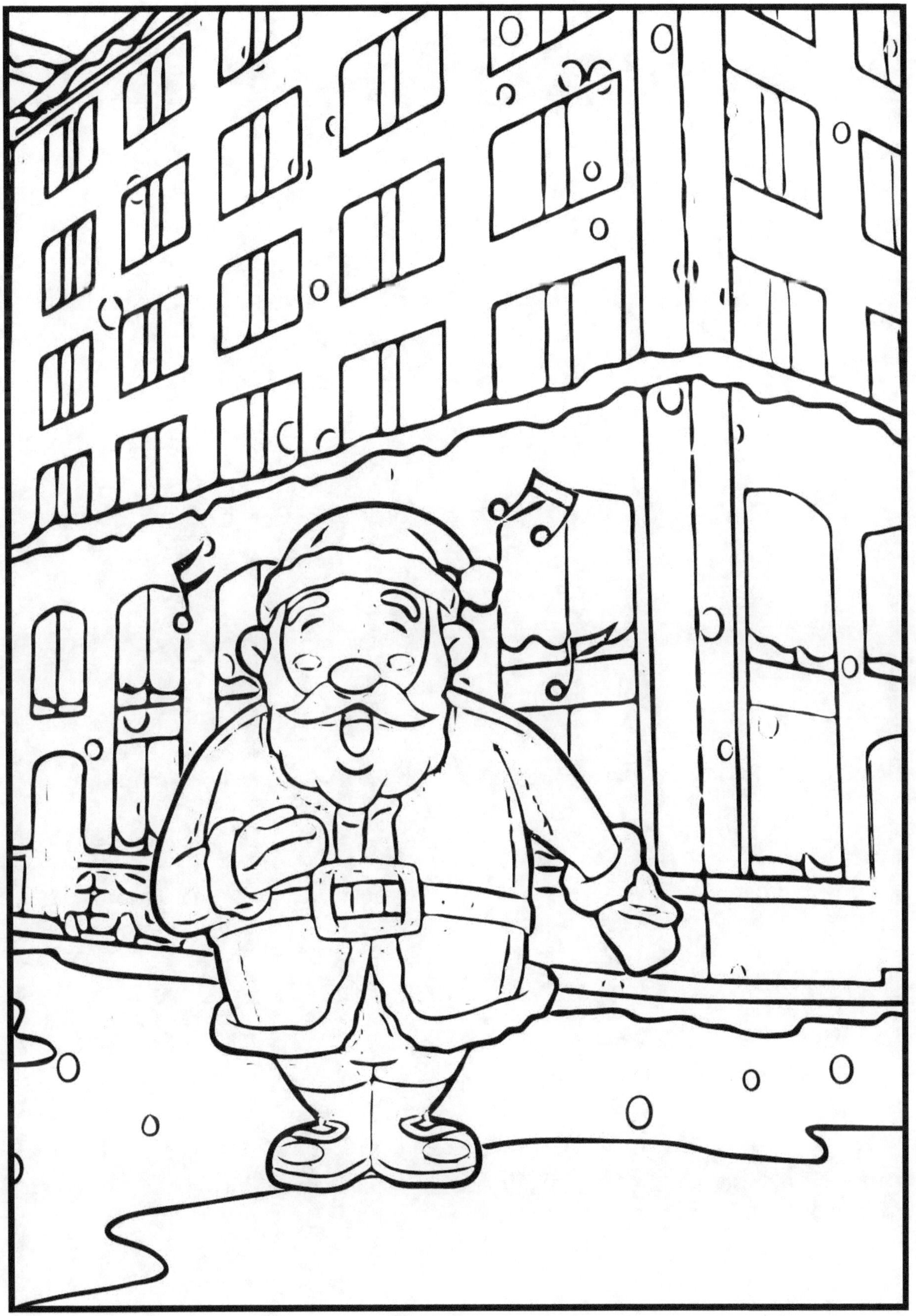

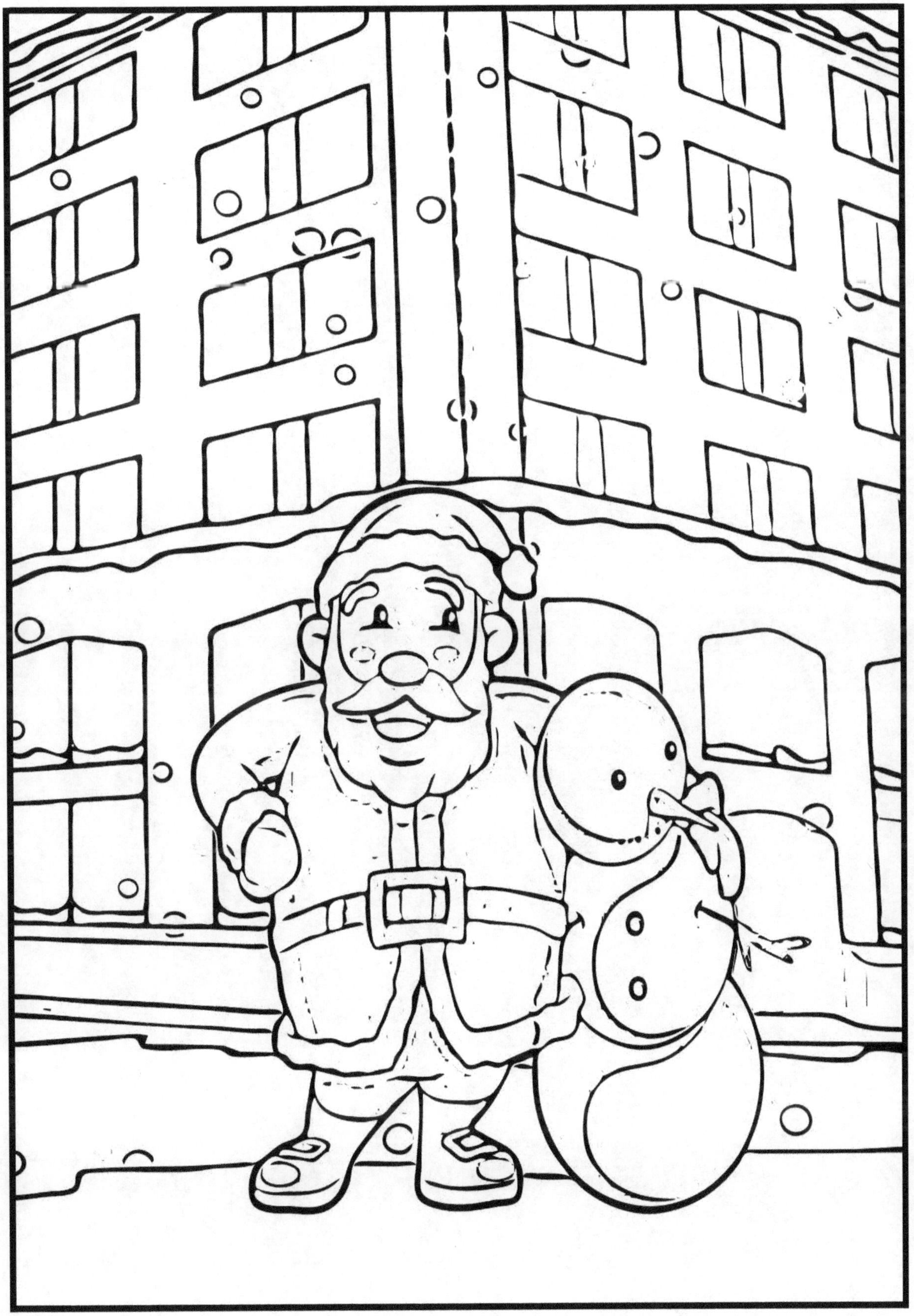

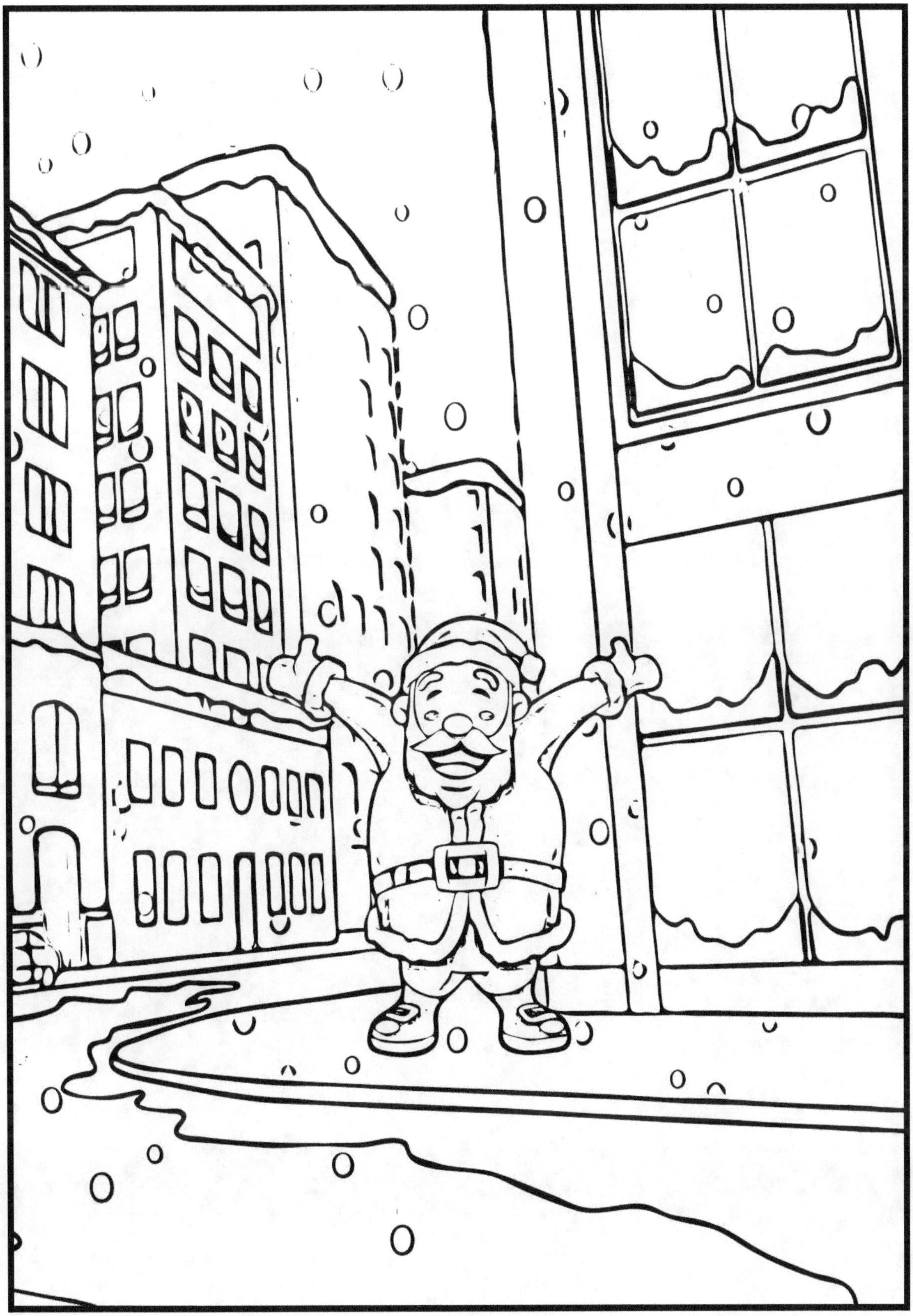

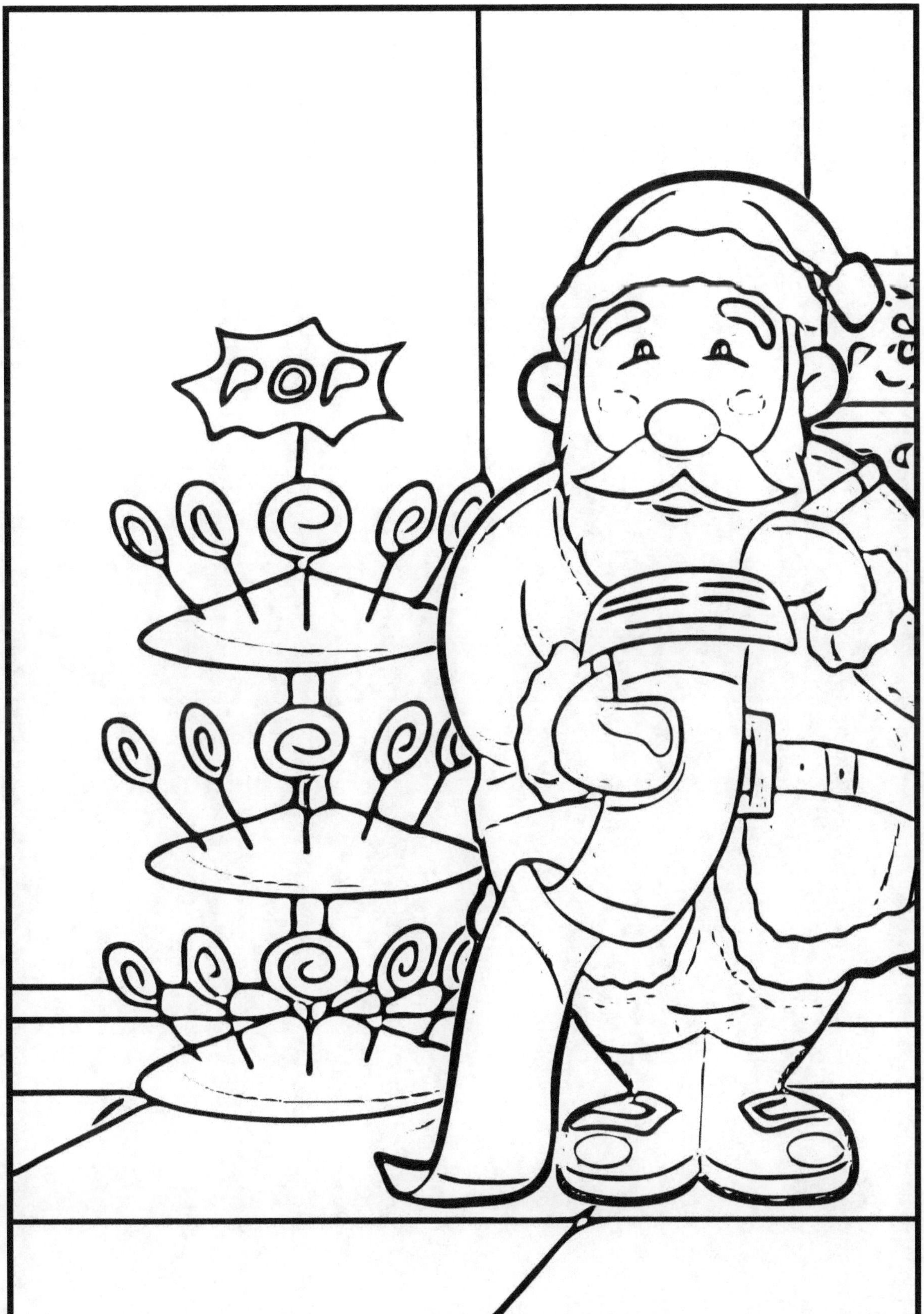
POP

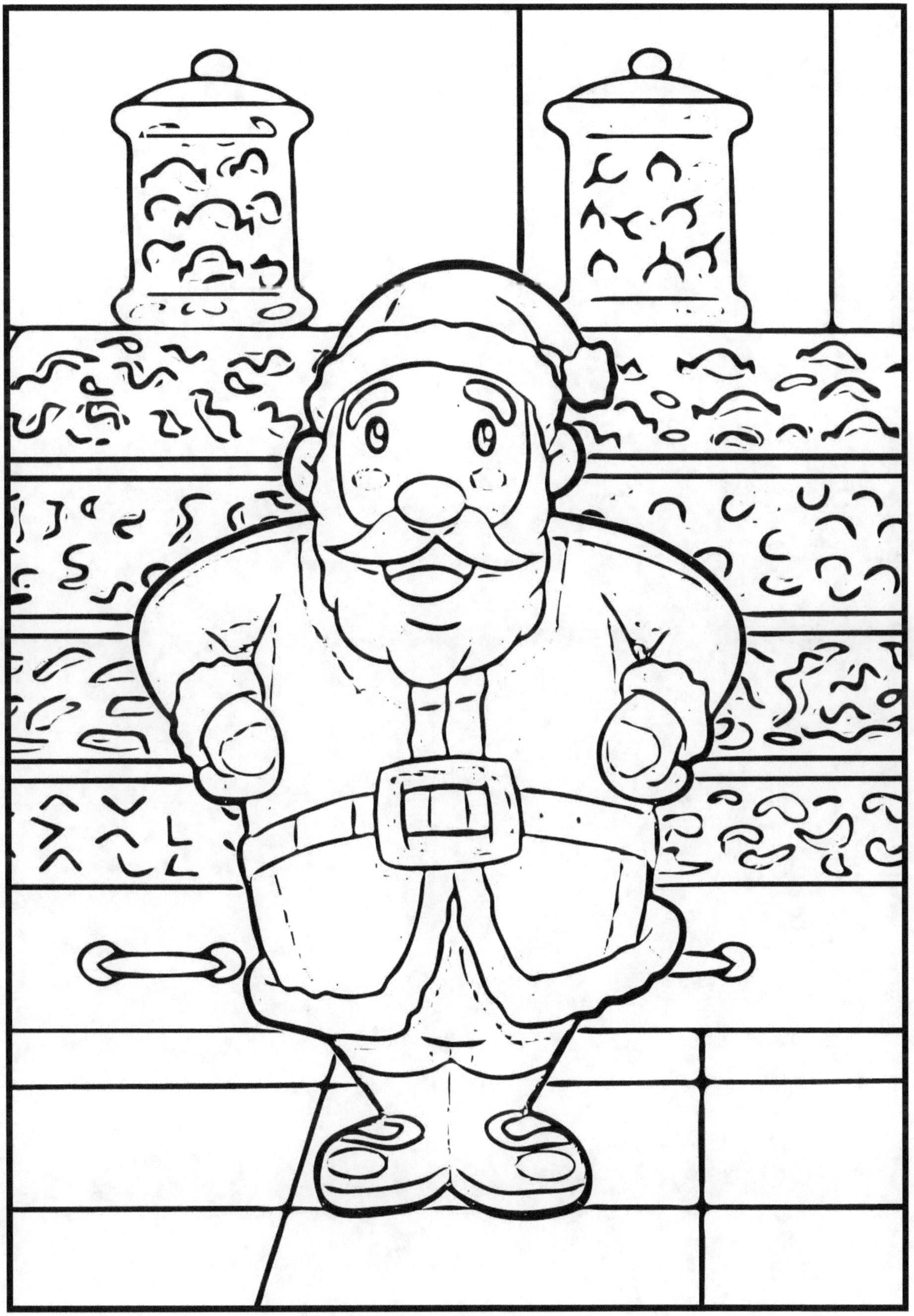

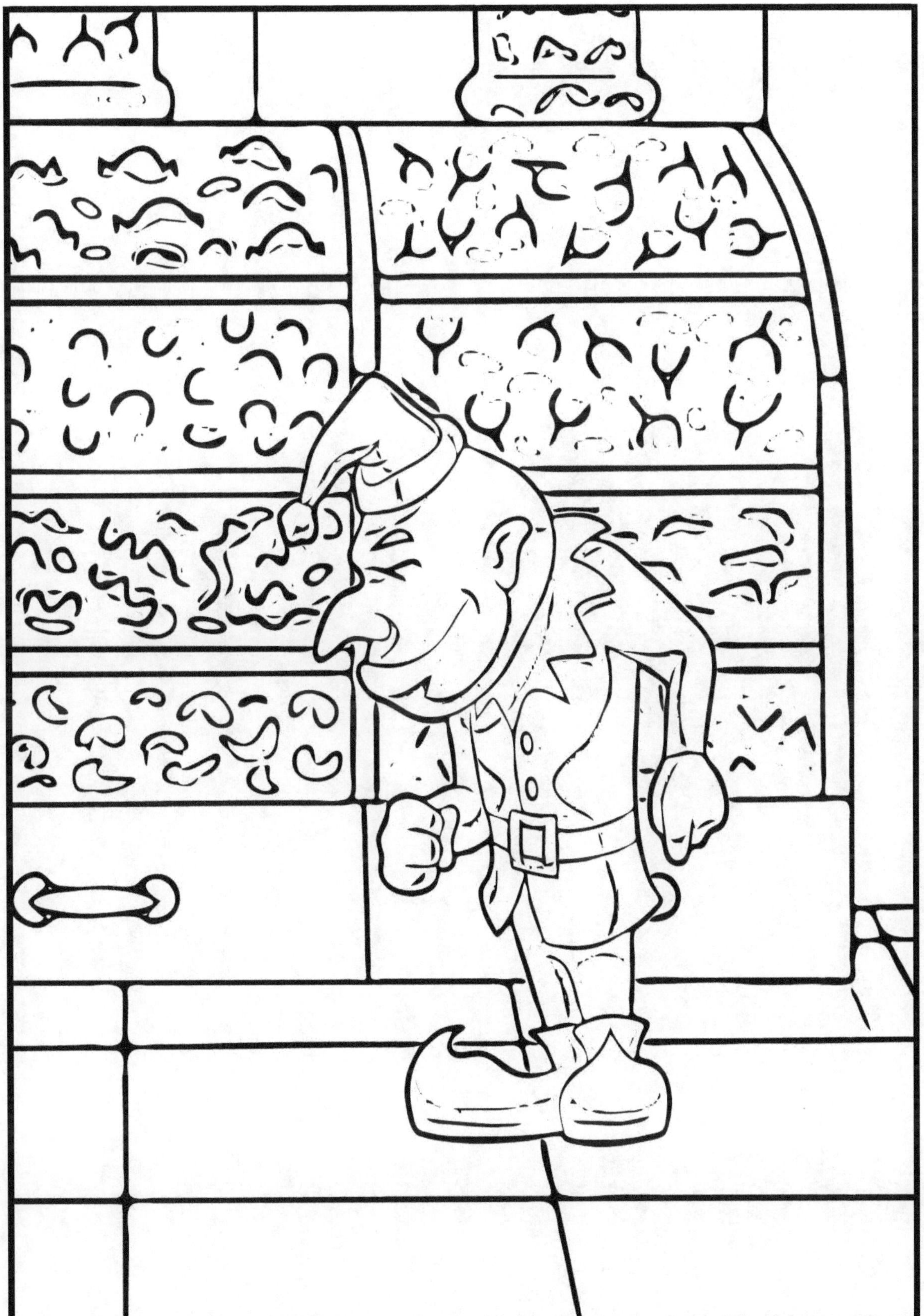

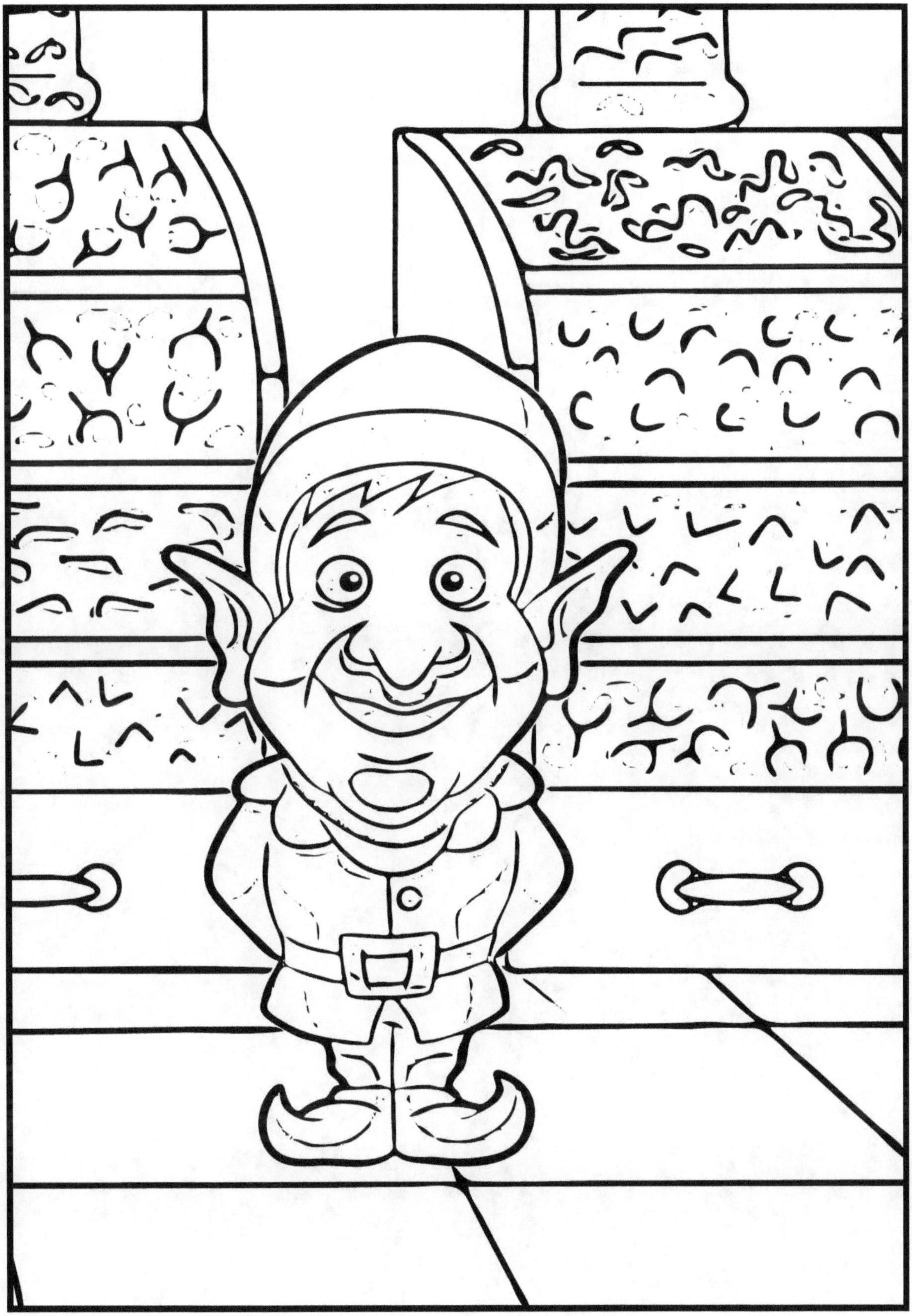

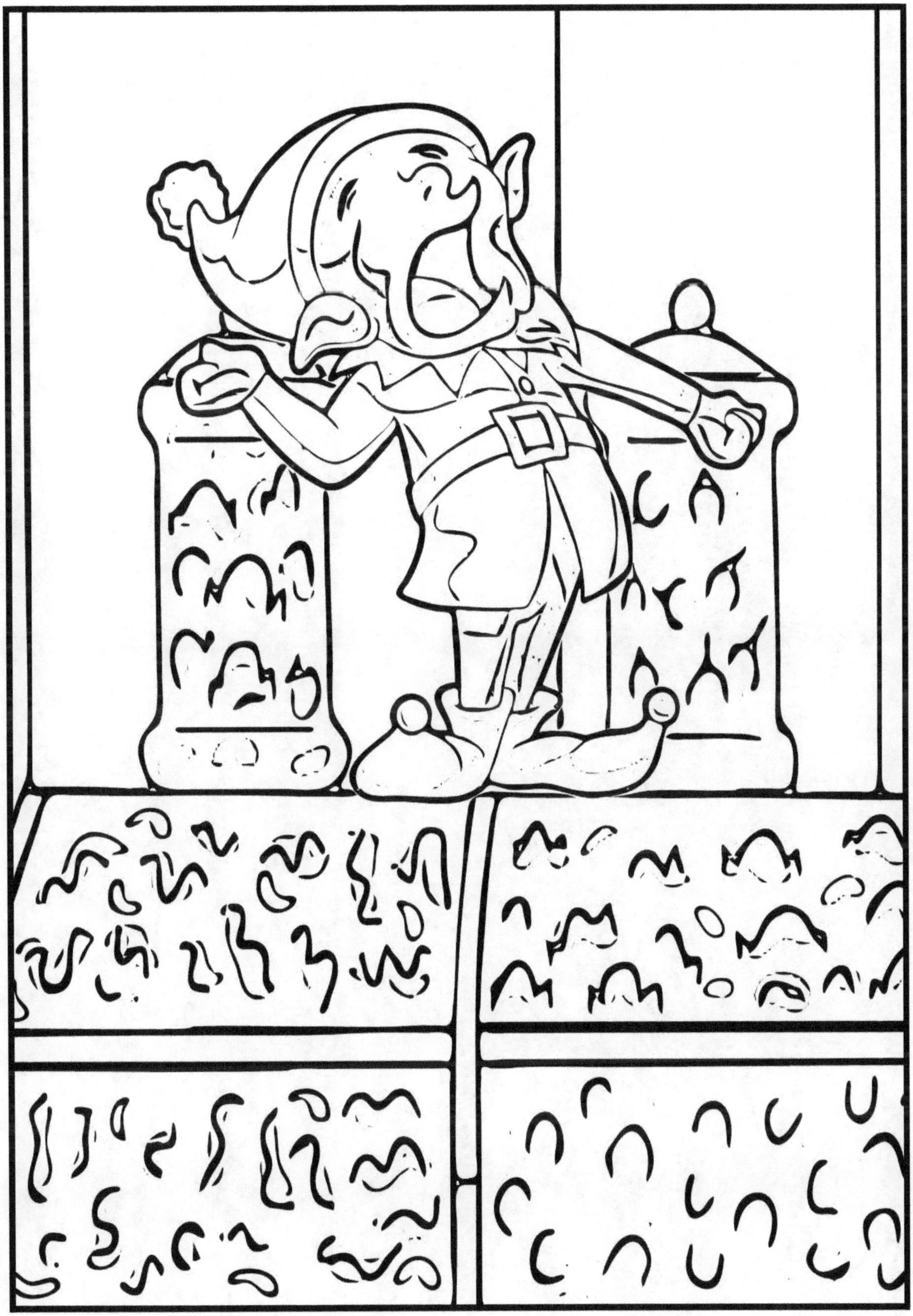

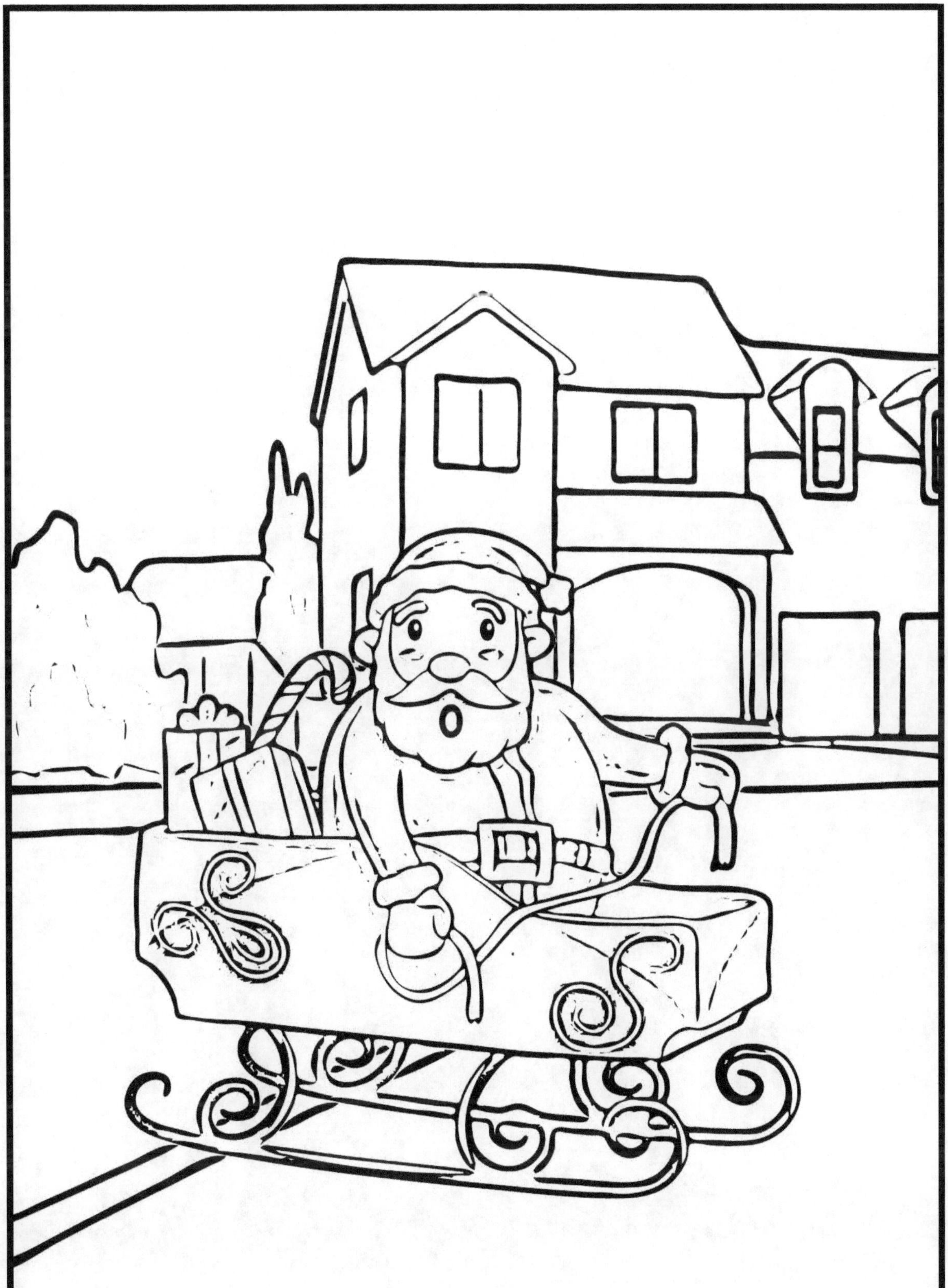

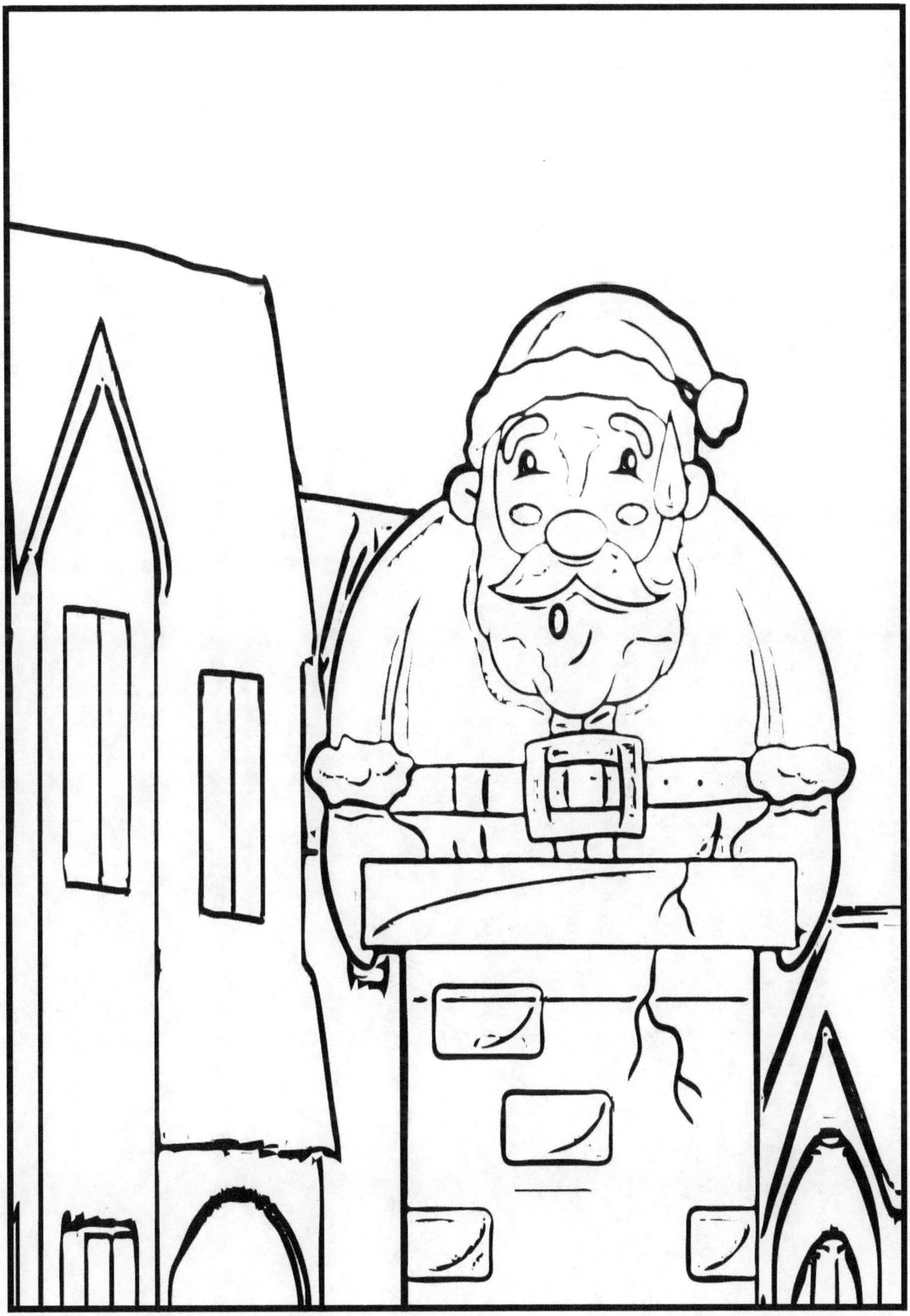

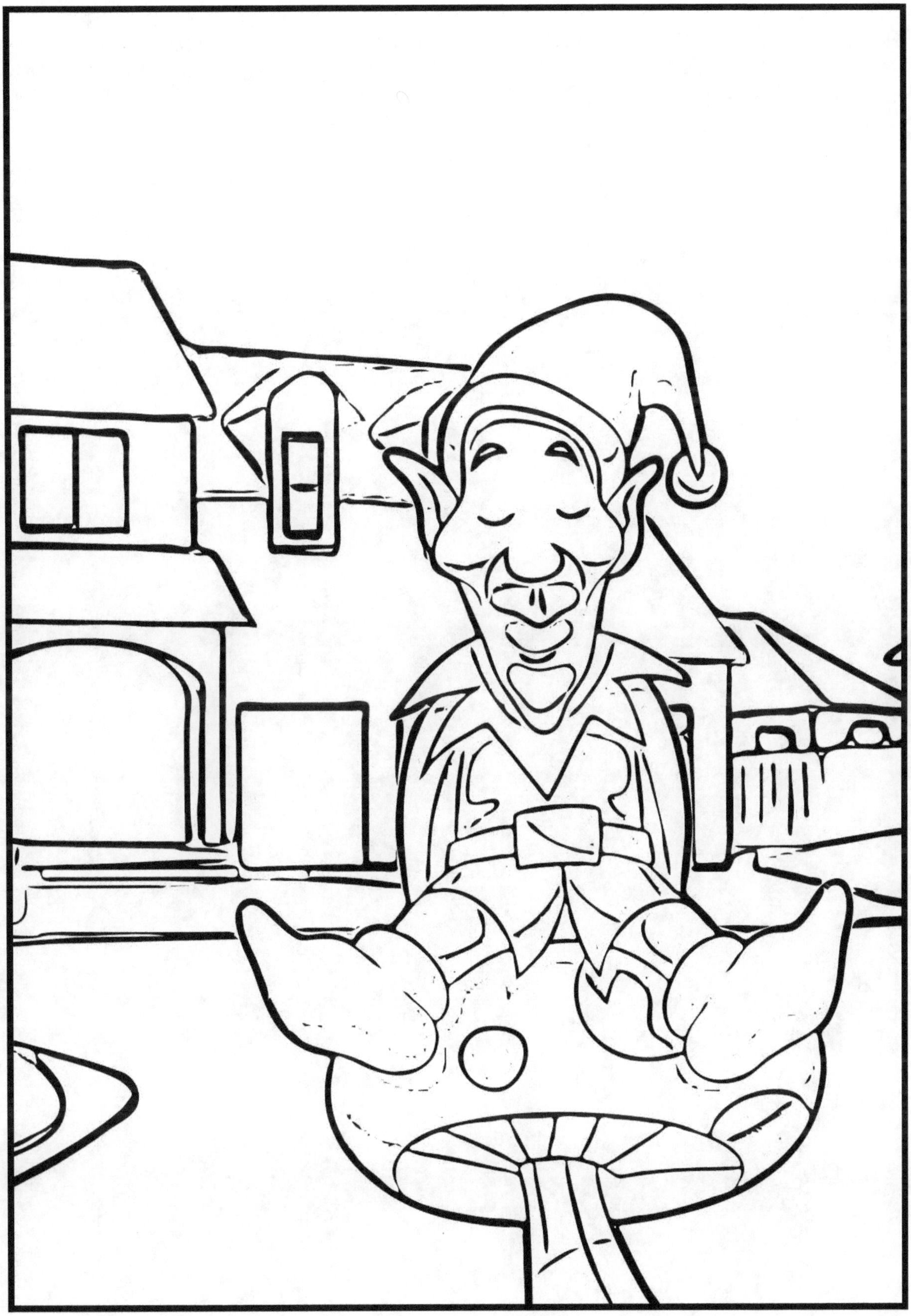

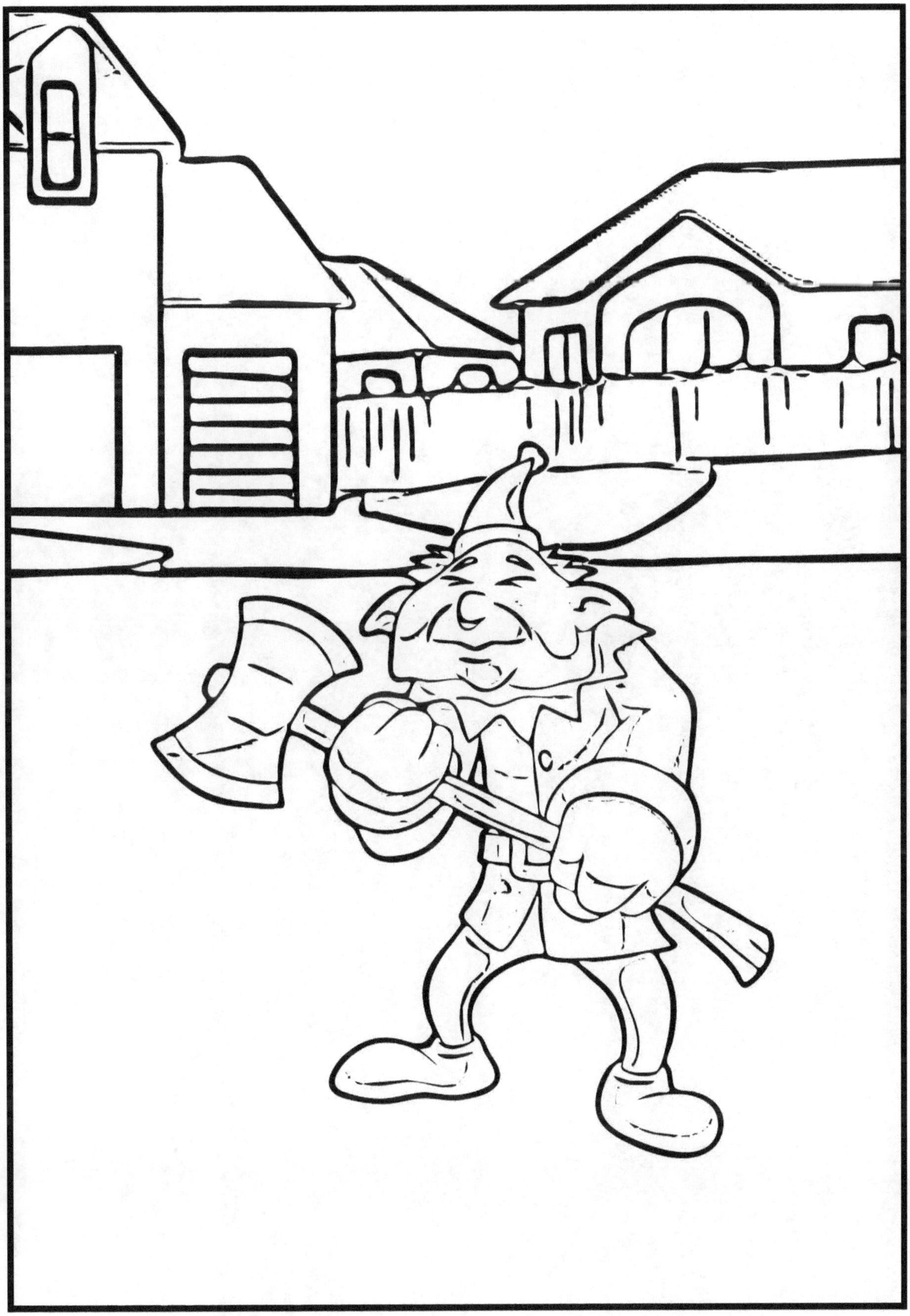

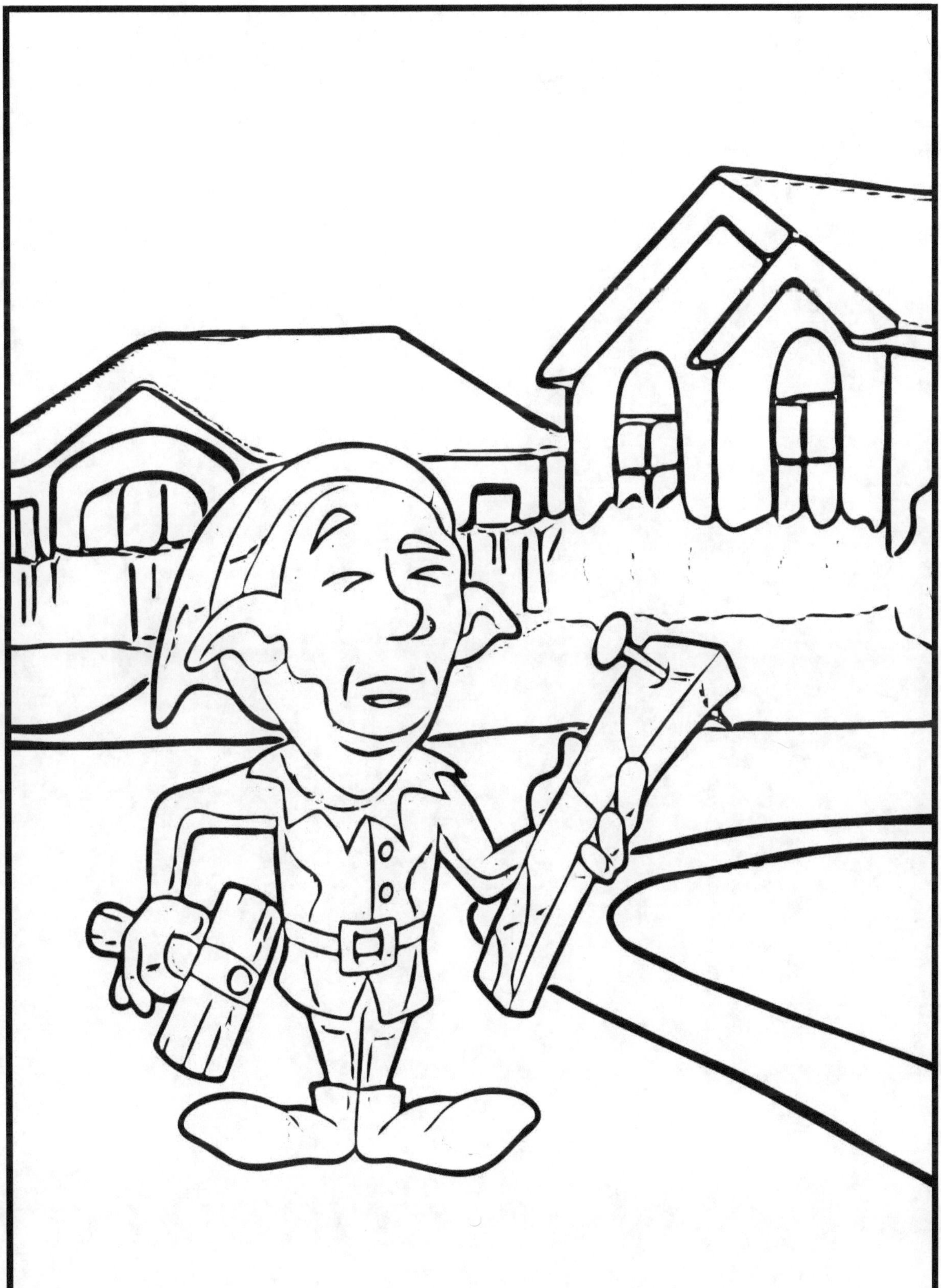

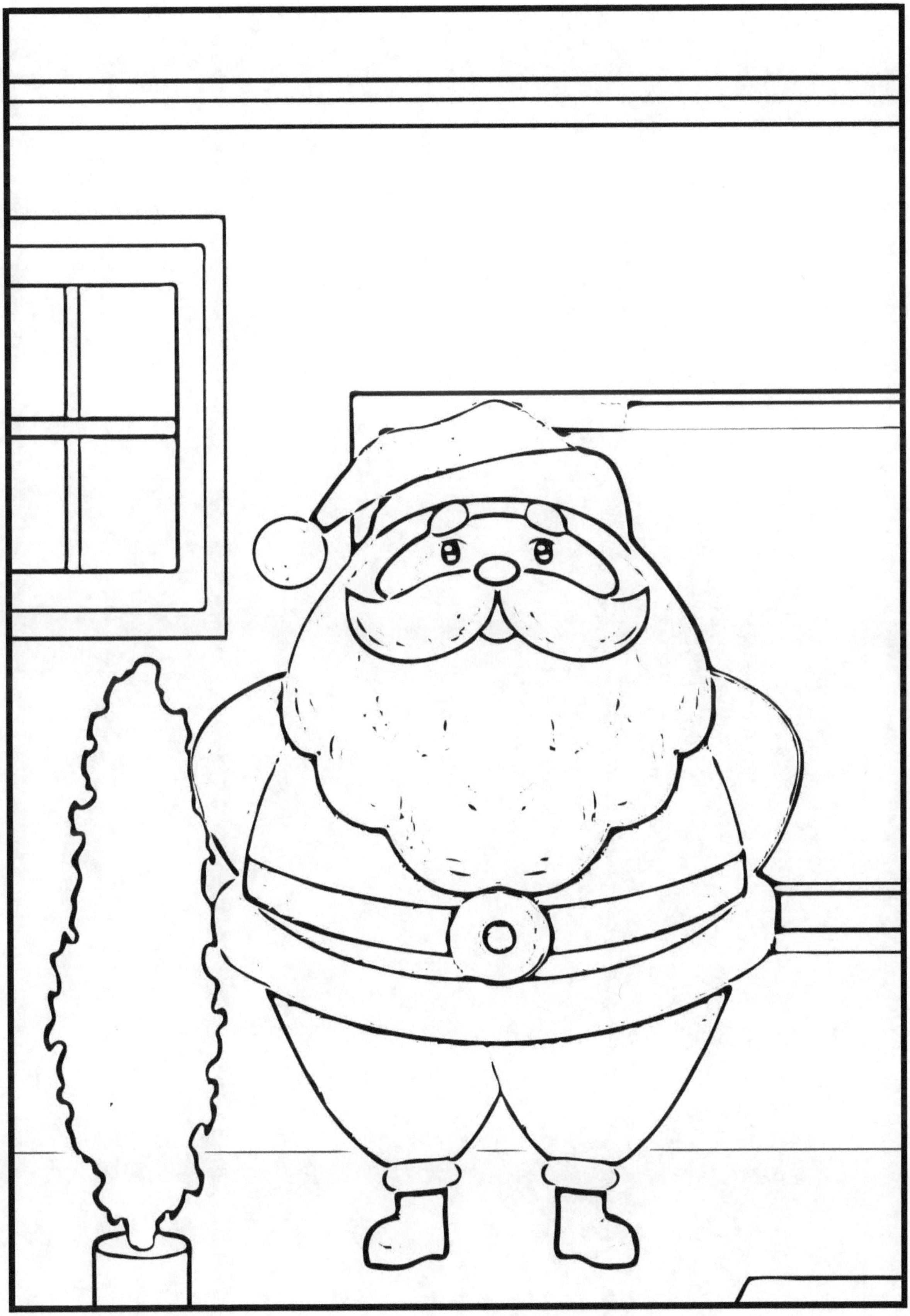

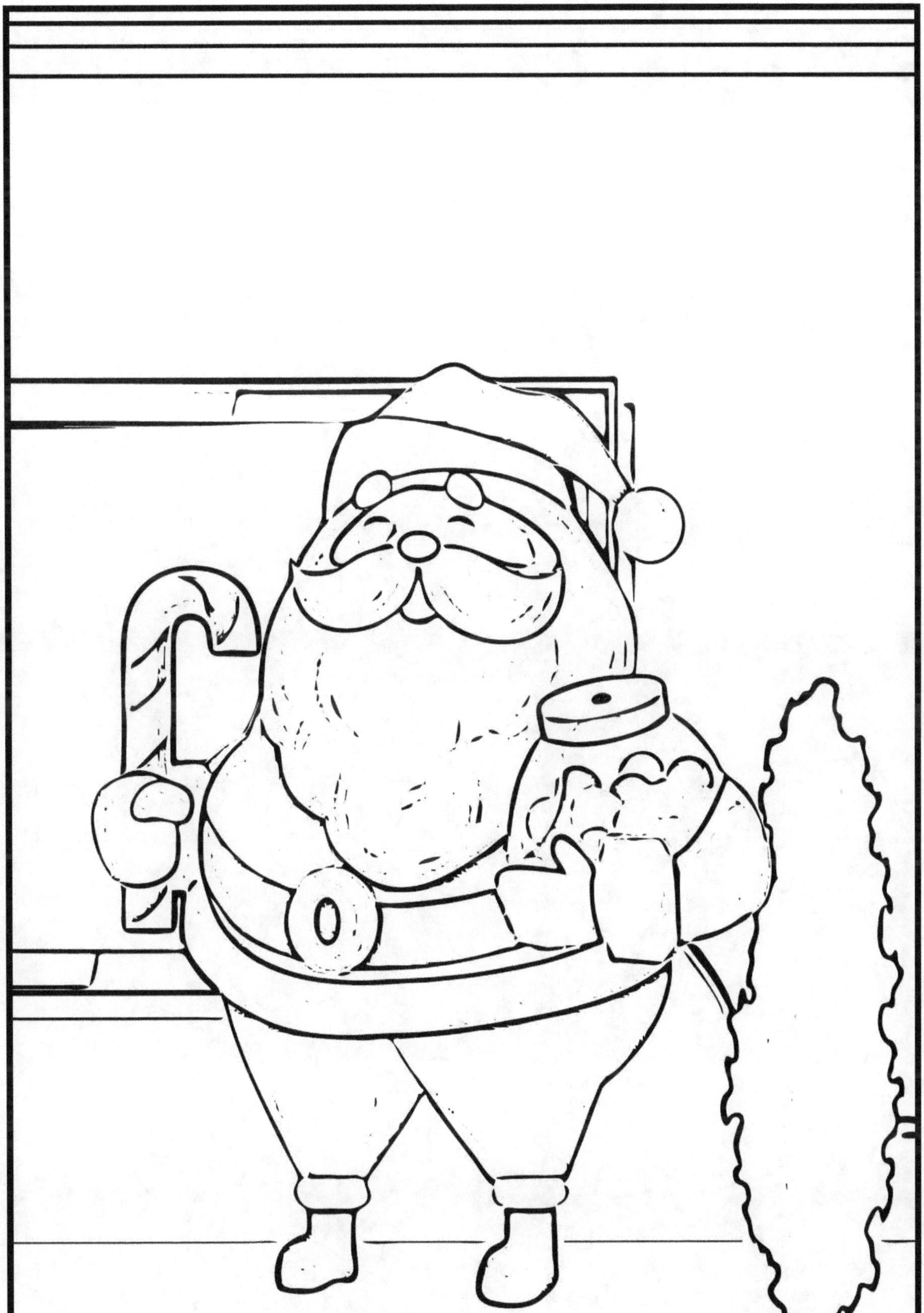

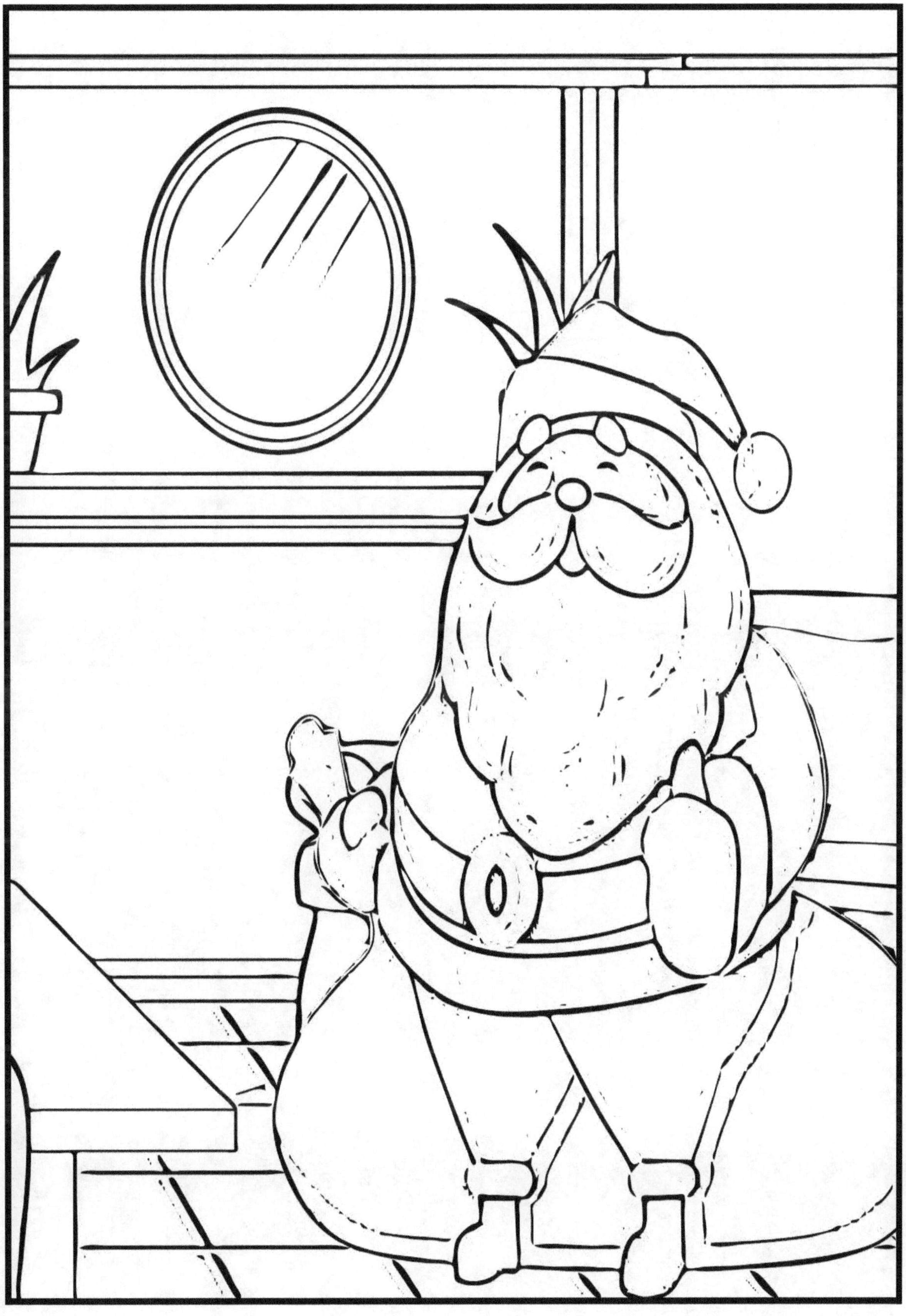

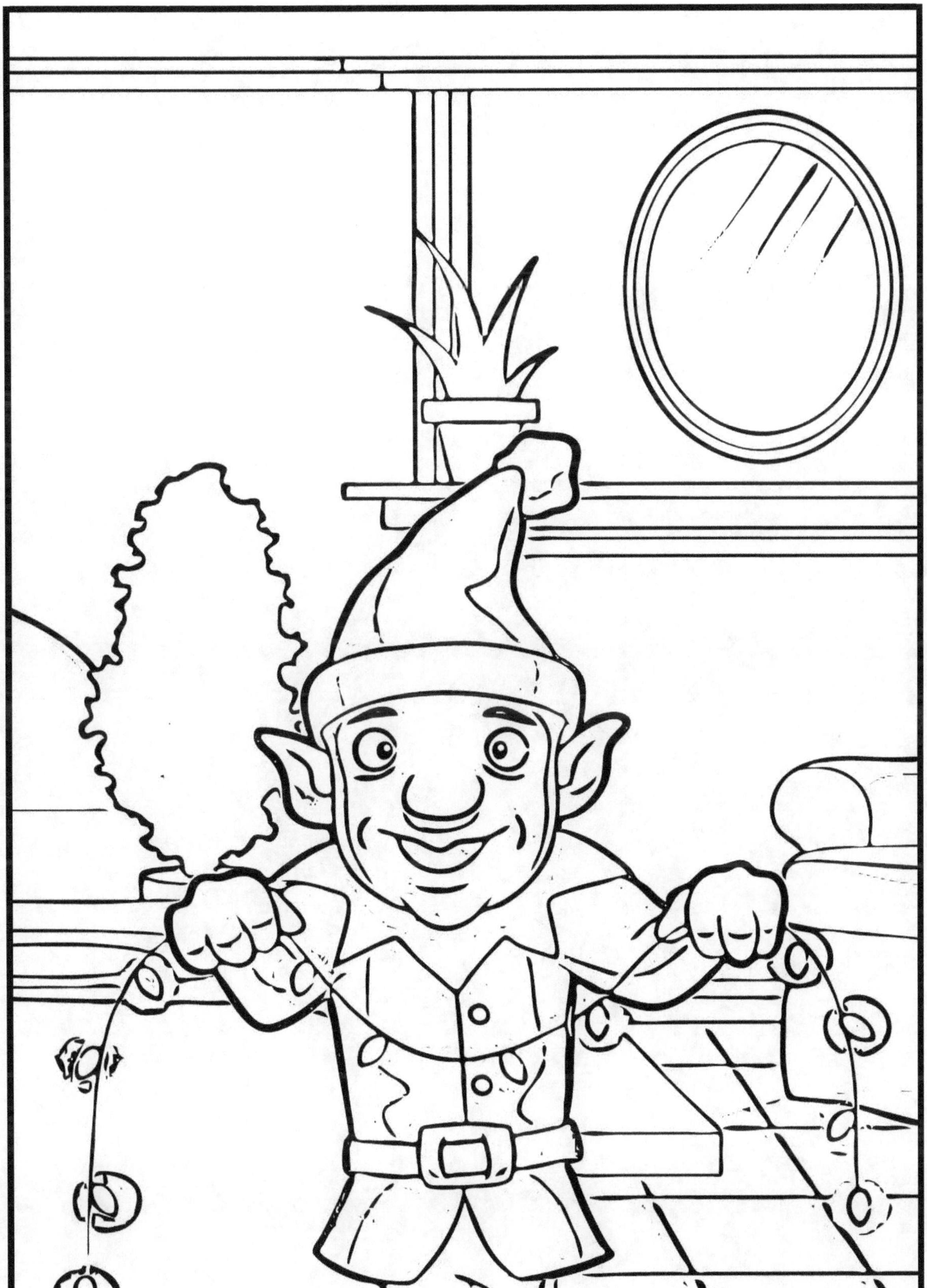

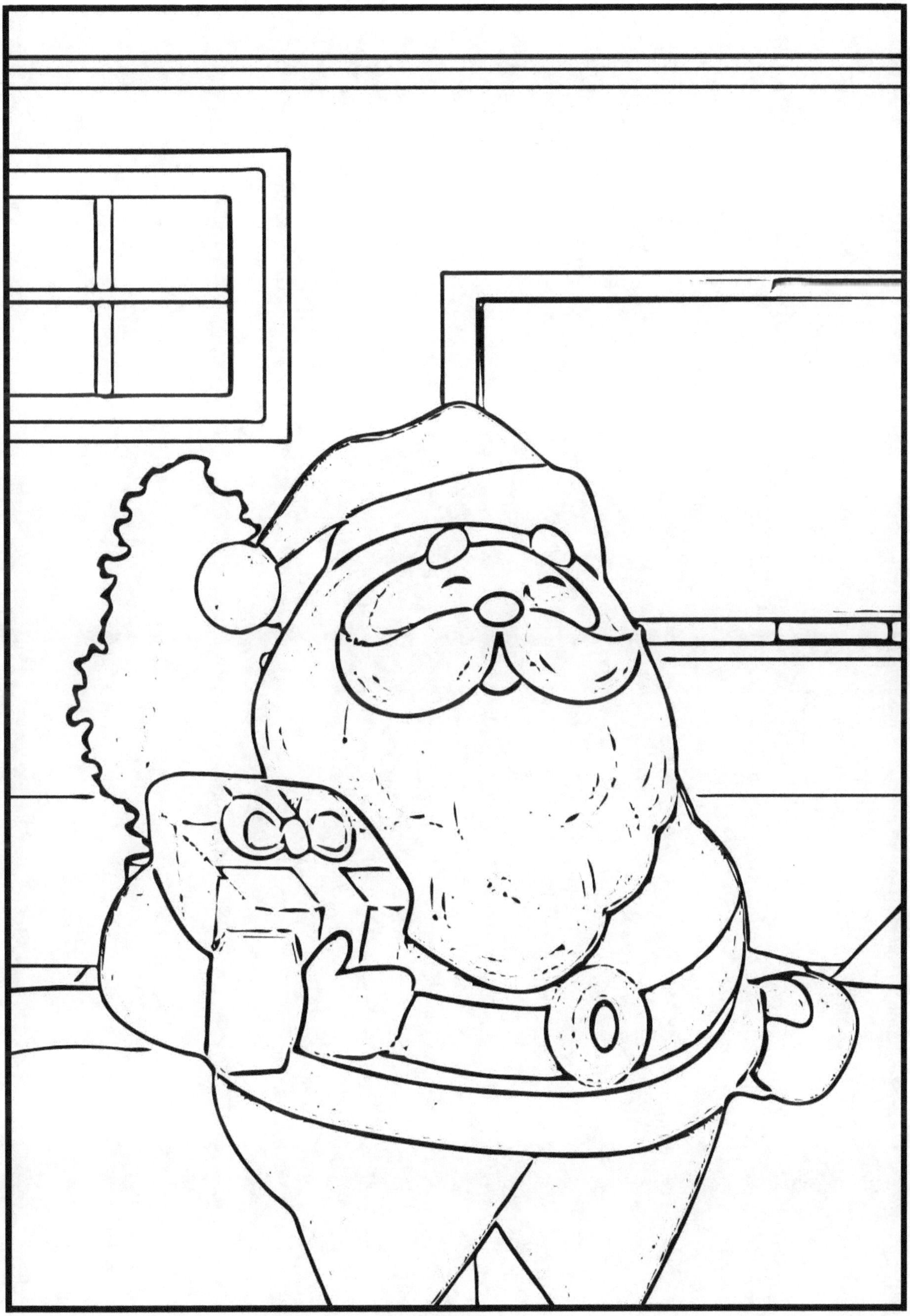

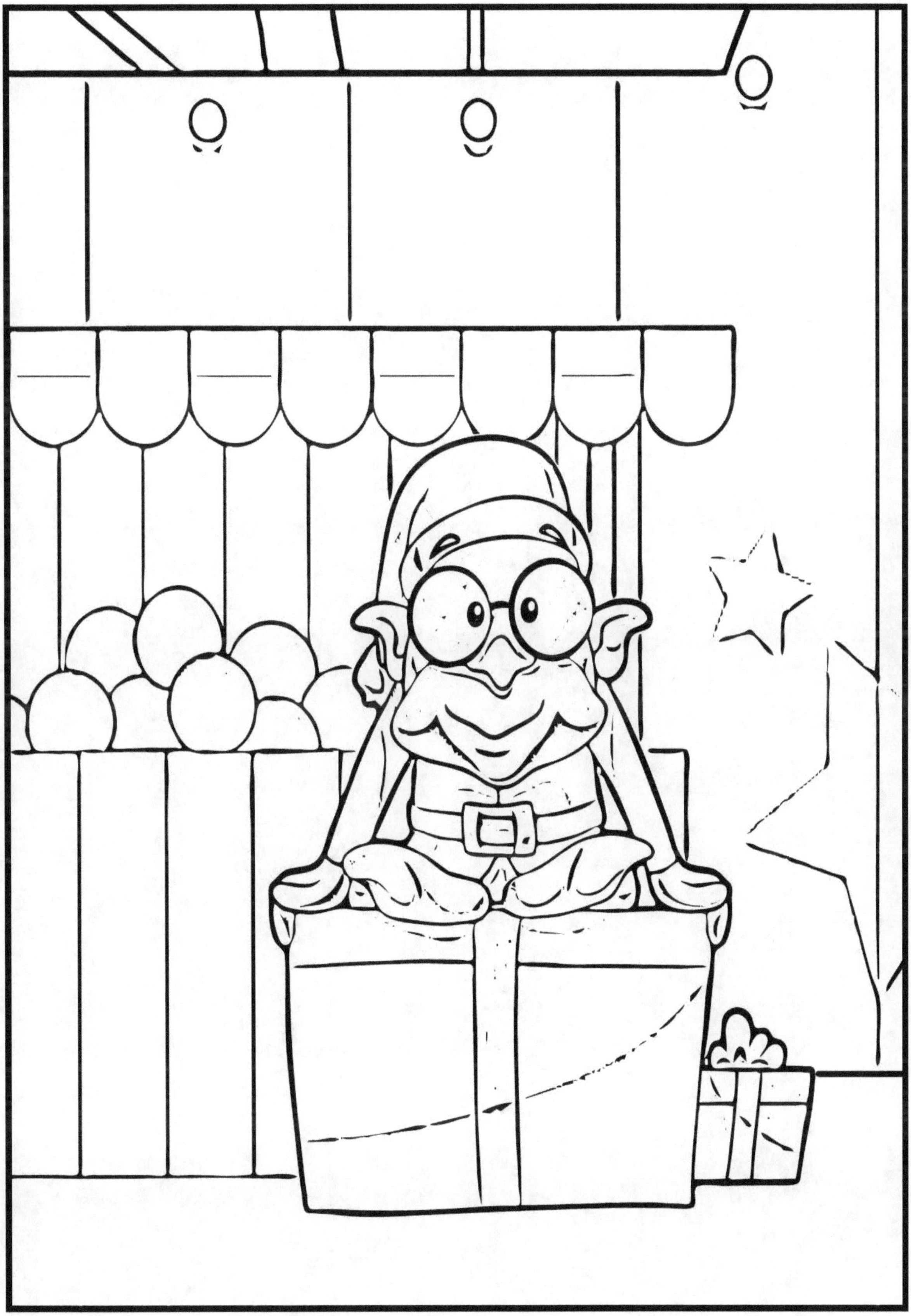

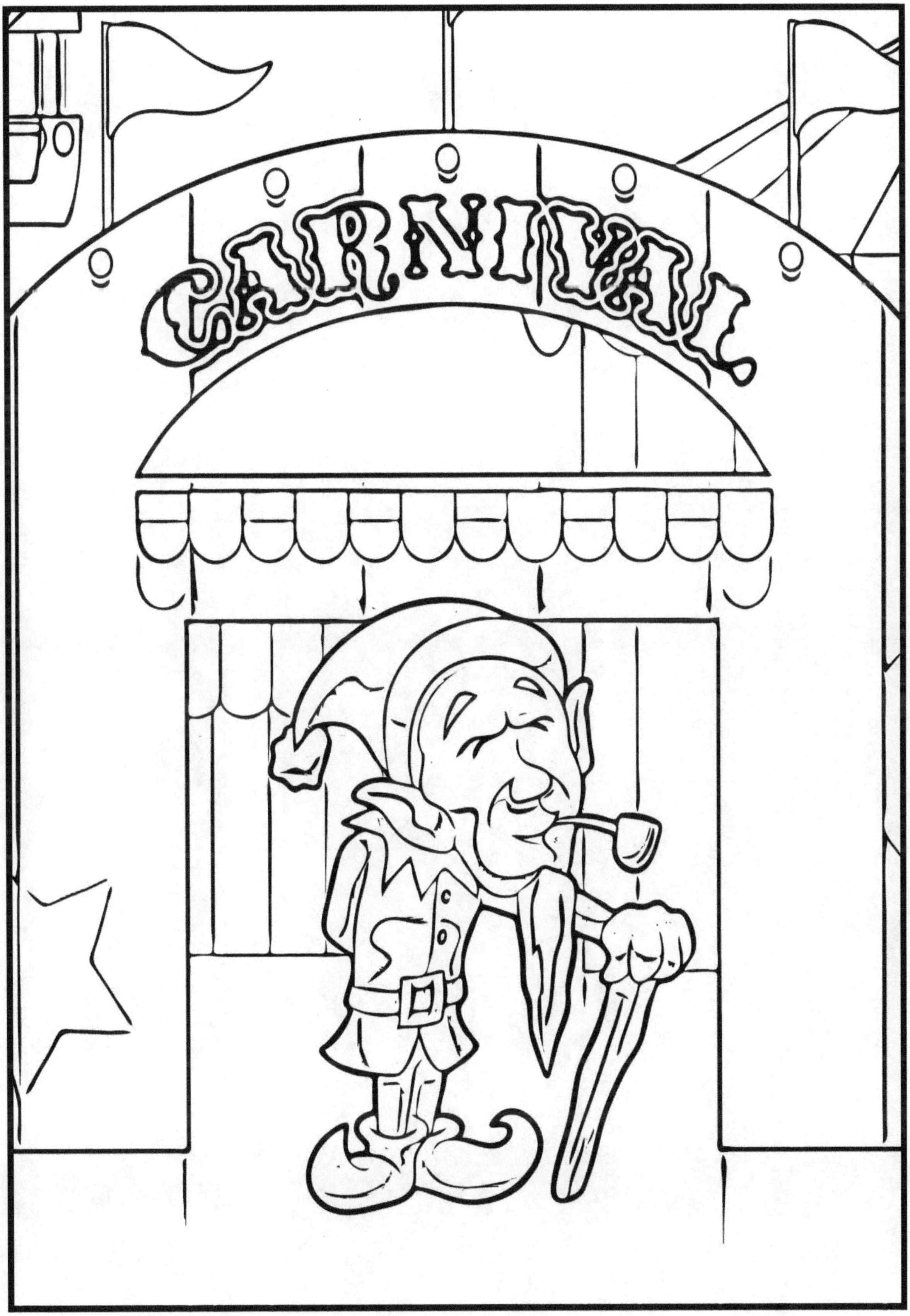
CARNIVAL

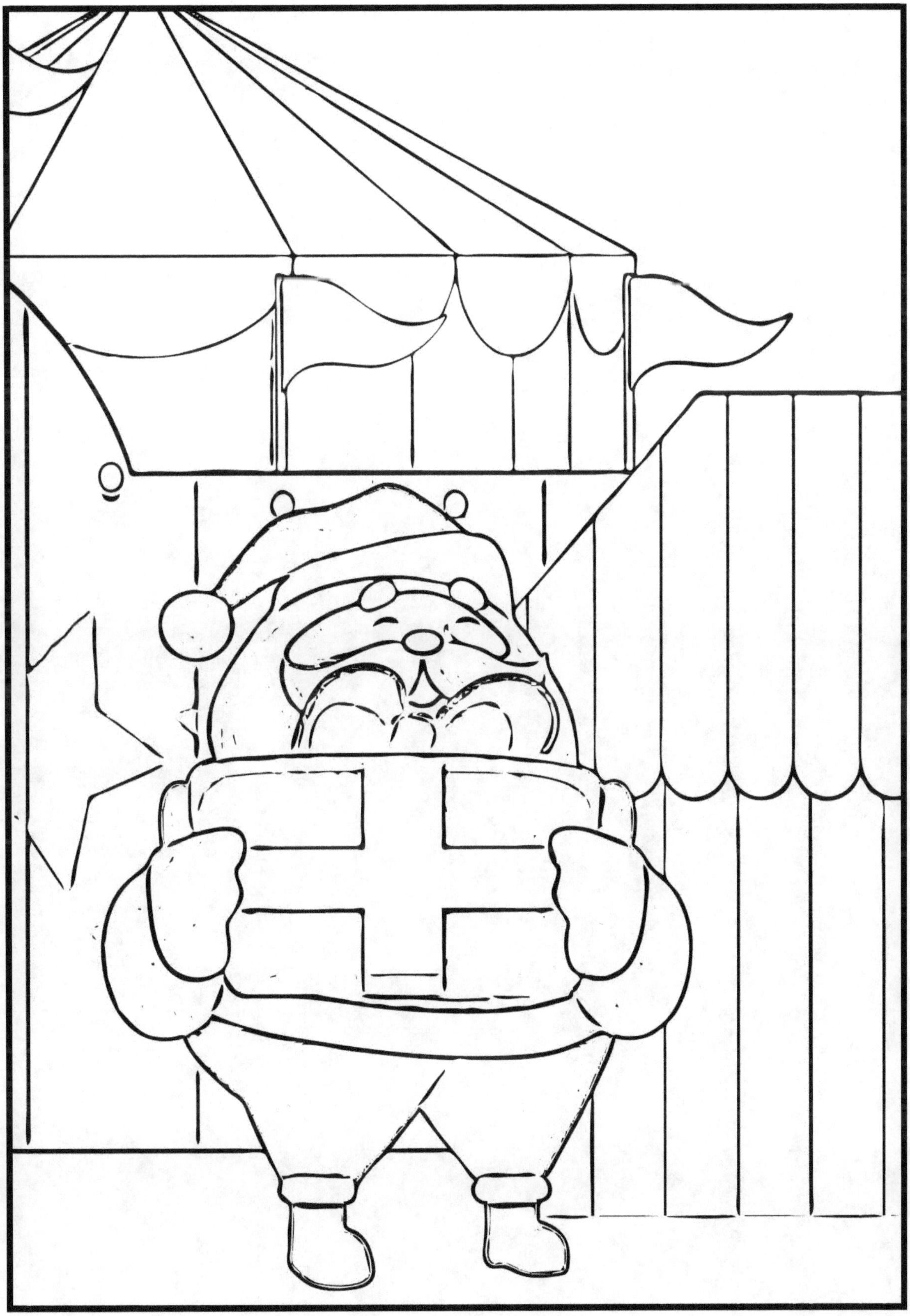

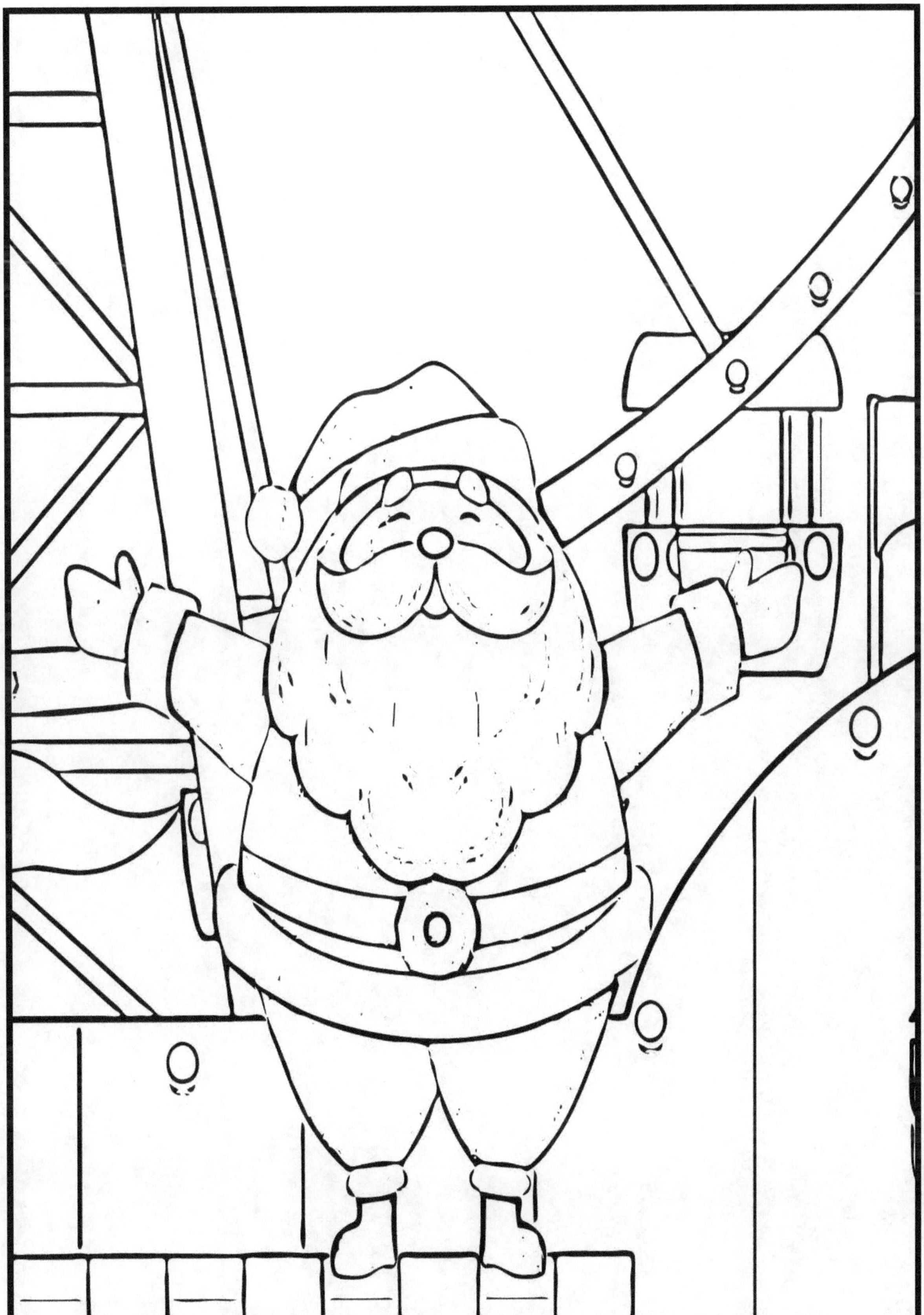

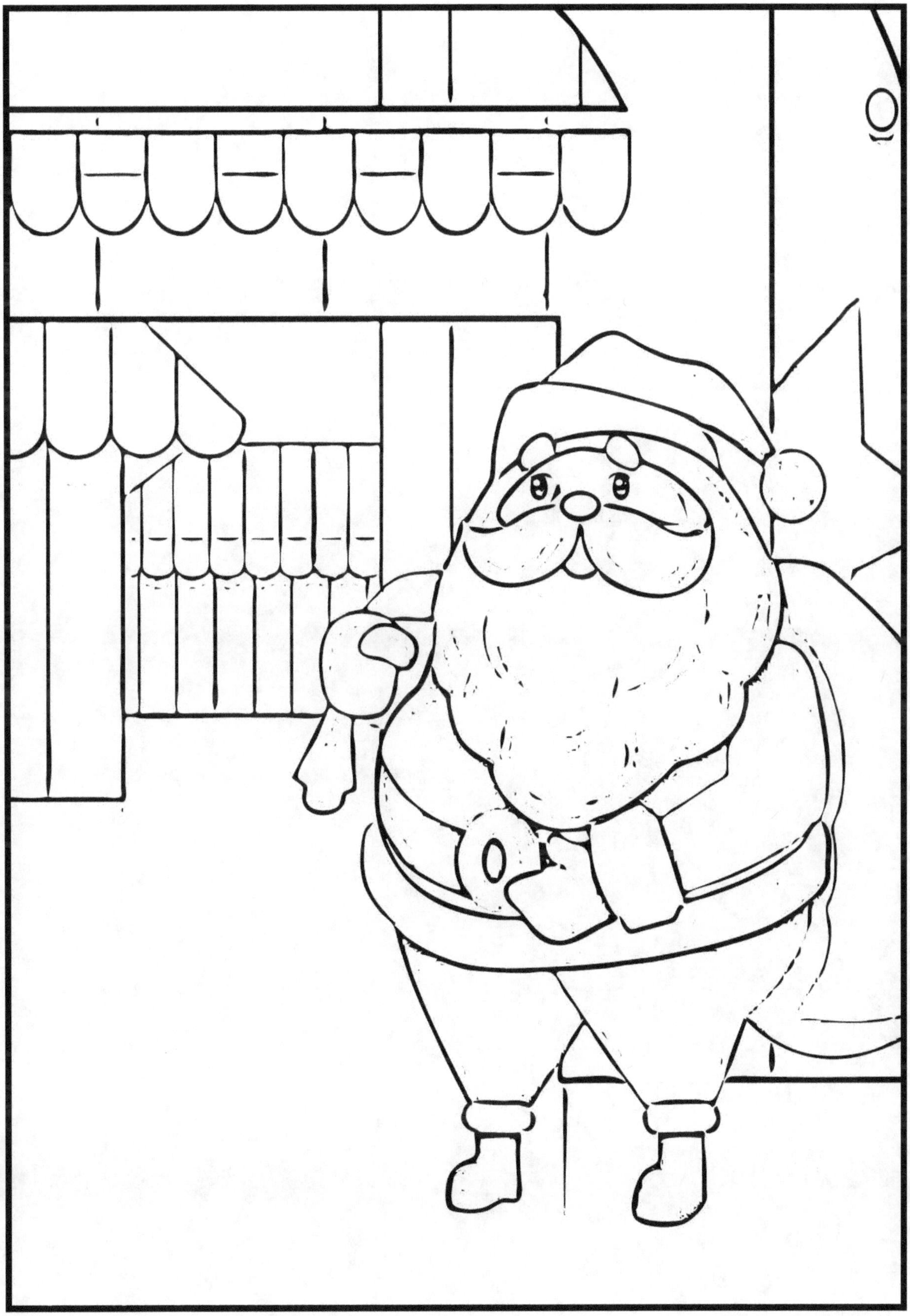

www.ingramcontent.com/pod-product-compliance
Lightning Source LLC
Chambersburg PA
CBHW080610180526
45168CB00007B/2849
9781518624506